Tony Gwynn

MR. PADRE

by
Barry Bloom

SPORTS PUBLISHING INC.
www.SportsPublishingInc.com

©1999 Sports Publishing Inc.
All rights reserved.

Book design, editor: Susan M. McKinney
Cover design: Scot Muncaster
Photos: *The Associated Press, San Diego State University*

ISBN: 1-58261-049-5
Library of Congress Catalog Card Number: 99-64489

SPORTS PUBLISHING INC.
804 N. Neil
Champaign, IL 61820
www.SportsPublishingInc.com

Printed in the United States.

CONTENTS

Tony has played his entire major-league career for the Padres. (AP/Wide World Photos)

Tony Visits the Monuments

After 16 years playing major league baseball, Tony Gwynn finally made it to Yankee Stadium.

Having grown up in southern California and playing his entire career in the National League with the San Diego Padres, Tony never had the opportunity to visit one of the great shrines of baseball history. He had played many games across New York at Shea Stadium, the ballpark in Flushing, Queens, that is home to the New York Mets. Shea isn't Yan-

Tony made his first visit to Yankee Stadium in 1998.
(AP/Wide World Photos)

kee Stadium, known for more than 70 years as The House That Ruth built.

It is 10 miles by car between the two ballparks spanning two boroughs, one bridge and two parkways. By subway, the two-hour trip is long and difficult, winding its way through mid-town Manhattan where passengers must change from the Flushing line to the Lexington Avenue line for the Bronx.

In baseball terms, the trip is also a hard one. Shea Stadium was built on a garbage dump and opened in 1964. Yankee Stadium opened in 1923 just across the river from the old Polo Grounds, the home of baseball's New York Giants. That stadium served for a time as the home of the Yankees, and in its final two years before it was torn down, was the home of the expansion Mets. The Yankees have won 24 World Series championships; the Mets have won two.

Tony, who understands and appreciates the history of the game he plays, knew about the sig-

Tony warms up before the 1998 World Series begins in 1998. (AP/Wide World Photos)

nificance of Yankee Stadium. So when his Padres won their second National League pennant in 1998, advancing to the World Series, it was with a special reverence that Tony prepared to make his first visit to Yankee Stadium.

The first two games were in New York. The Stadium had changed a great deal since Babe Ruth hit a home run in the first game there, having been renovated in the 1970s, but that didn't matter to Tony.

The day before the opening game is reserved for workouts, and Tony awoke early and left the team hotel with Anthony, his 16-year-old son. They decided to take the subway north through east Harlem and into the Bronx. They entered the stadium through an outfield gate, and instead of heading directly to the visiting clubhouse, they walked toward the famed Monument Garden beyond the left-center field fence. Tony was so much in awe that he made the trip twice.

Tony has a great appreciation for the history of baseball.
(AP/Wide World Photos)

That first time, he wanted to see the monuments in private, without the pressure of the media watching him. A Yankee Stadium guard almost kept Tony from the area until he recognized him.

Later, as the Padres took batting practice, a television crew and several reporters went along as Tony again looked at the tributes to all of the great Yankees of the past. It occurred to Tony that the Yankees had already won 20 World Championships before the Padres' franchise was born in 1969.

"It's impressive," Tony said. "So many great players. So much history." Tony stood in front of the original three monuments honoring Ruth, Lou Gehrig and manager Miller Huggins. "And the way they have it done, wow, there are some museums that aren't this plush."

In the Garden, the retired numbers of 15 Yankees players rest on a bank of flowers just below the

Tony receives congratulations from teammate Andy Ashby after another of Tony's game-winning hits. (AP/ Wide World Photos)

bullpens, including Roger Maris (9), Mickey Mantle (7), and Reggie Jackson (44). The original three monuments are set aside just as they once were around the flag pole. Before the stadium was renovated in 1972, those monuments and the flag pole were on the field—460-feet away from home plate.

"I had no idea that was the home run wall back there," Tony said. "You learn something new about the game every year you play. This place kind of reminds me of the Hall of Fame. You walk into that room and see the plaques honoring all the great players who have played the game. There's only something like 200 players in there. You realize it's something to make the Hall of Fame."

When Tony began playing baseball, he could only dream about places like Yankee Stadium and the Hall of Fame.

Tony (at left) and his younger brother, Chris Gwynn. (AP/Wide World Photos)

2

Growing Up

Tony grew up in Long Beach, California—not far from downtown Los Angeles. He went to college at San Diego State, almost as far away from New York as one can get and still be in the United States.

Tony was the second oldest of three boys in a close-knit, working class family. Tony considered his mom, Vendella, a postal employee, the glue of his family, and his dad Charles, who worked in shipping and receivng for the state of California, the rock. Tony preceded younger brother Chris as a

Tony played baseball for the Aztecs of San Diego State University as a walk on. (San Diego State University)

baseball player at San Diego State and in the majors. Years later, in 1996, the only season the two played together with the Padres, Chris got the extra-inning, extra-base hit in the season's final game against the Dodgers that won only the Padres' second National League West title.

How important was dad to the two baseball-playing boys? When Tony broke his wrist as a Padres rookie, dad was on the phone to commiserate. When Jack Clark ripped Tony during a clubhouse meeting in the visitor's locker room at Shea Stadium, calling Tony a selfish player who cared more about his batting average than winning, Tony's dad was so fighting mad he told his son to stand his ground.

Tony graduated from Long Beach Polytechnic High School but was not drafted by a baseball team after his senior year. That was OK with Tony, because he had his mind set on going to college any-

Tony received a basketball scholarship to San Diego State University. (Photo by Ernie Anderson/San Diego State University)

way. He decided to go to San Diego State, where he received a basketball scholarship and he would have the opportunity to play baseball as a walk on. Two other schools would have made Tony pick one sport.

Tony had great success in both sports. He was a point guard on the San Diego State basketball team and is still the only athlete in Western Athletic Conference history to be named an all-conference performer in two sports. Tony also holds the Aztec assists record and was the 10th-round pick of the National Basketball Association's old San Diego Clippers on the same day in June 1981 he was picked in the third round of the baseball draft by the Padres.

It was also at San Diego State that Tony met his future wife, Alicia. She was on the track team in college. They have two children, a son, Anthony, and a daughter, Anisha.

Tony played point guard on the basketball team at San Diego State. (San Diego State University)

Tony's son Anthony prefers basketball over baseball, but baseball has always been Tony's sport. Standing only 5-foot-11, Tony was realistic enough to know he didn't have much of a future competing against much more imposing players.

Anthony plays high school basketball with the son of former Padres and Cardinals shortstop Garry Templeton. During his trip to New York for the World Series, Tony said his son was more concerned about the National Basketball Association lockout delaying the start of the regular season.

"He's a basketball guy," Tony said. "He's upset the pro players are locked out now, but he knows what all this is all about. We talk about it all the time. That's one of the great things about getting to play here."

When Tony realized his dream of signing a professional contract, he wasn't worried about money or lockouts or anything negative. All he was asking was a chance, and the Padres were giving it to him.

Tony was an all-conference selection in both basketball and baseball while at San Diego State. (San Diego State University)

The Minors

Tony played his first professional game in Walla Walla, Washington, in 1981. The team is in the rookie-level Northwest League, and was the starting place for many future Padres, including shortstop Ozzie Smith.

It took only 42 games at Walla Walla for Padres officials to realize that Tony was ready to play against tougher competition. He hit 12 homers, drove in 37 runs and won the league batting title with a .331 average, earning MVP honors in the league as well as a promotion to Double A Amarillo, Texas.

Tony rose quickly through the Padres' minor-league system. (AP/Wide World Photos)

The jump of two levels within the San Diego organization didn't slow Tony down. In fact, he did better at the higher level. In 23 games at the end of the season, Tony hit .462 with four homers and 19 RBI.

As he rested that winter, Tony had plenty of reasons to be pleased. He had shown he could play and play well at the professional level, and even if he had to start the 1982 season back at Double A, he knew he had shown Padres' officials that he was somebody they needed to be following closely.

The Padres were indeed well aware of Tony, and decided that it was time to see what he could do at the highest level of the farm system, at Triple A Hawaii in the Pacific Coast League. Again, Tony was ready for the challenge. In 93 games, he hit .328, with five homers and 46 RBI. With the Padres headed for a fourth-place finish in the NL West, it was time to see if Tony was ready for the majors.

Along with country singer Garth Brooks, Gwynn is part of the charitable "Touch'em All" foundation for kids. (AP/Wide World Photos)

Ready for the Majors

On July 19, 1982, Tony was in the Padres' lineup for their game against the Phillies. If he was nervous or apprehensive, he didn't let it show. He calmly collected the first two hits of his major-league career.

Tony got at least one hit in 15 consecutive games, the longest streak on the Padres that season. It wasn't an opposing pitcher who stopped him but a broken left wrist, suffered when he dove for a fly ball in the outfield in Pittsburgh on August 25.

Tony waits for his turn in the batting cage before a game in San Diego. (AP/Wide World Photos)

Another broken wrist interrupted Tony's season in the Puerto Rican Winter League, and got his 1983 season off to a slow start. He played 17 games at Triple A Las Vegas as part of a rehabilitation assignment, then rejoined the major-league club.

For the first time in his career, Tony was struggling at the plate. He hit just .233 in his first 24 games in San Diego, but then found his groove again. Over the final 62 games of the season, Tony's average was .333, improving his mark for the year to .309, the first of his many years above .300. From August 11 to September 26, Tony got at least one hit in 39 of the Padres' 41 games, including 25 games in a row, at the time the Padres' longest hitting streak in history and the longest in the majors in 1983.

Tony was poised to do even better the next year.

CHAPTER FIVE

A Batting Title and a Pennant

Surrounded by veteran players such as Steve Garvey, Goose Gossage and Graig Nettles, the 24-year-old Tony was not the player the Padres expected to be the star of the team in 1984. He got off to a quick start, however, and neither he nor the team ever looked back.

Tony won his first career batting title with a .351 average. He led all of baseball with 213 hits and 69 multiple-hit games. He became the first Padre to record 200 or more hits in a season, break-

Tony falls to the ground after being hit in the leg by a pitch from Chicago Cubs pitcher Mark Clark. (AP/Wide World Photos)

ing the team record of 194 set by Gene Richards. He was voted into the starting lineup for his first All-Star game, at Candlestick Park in San Francisco, and finished third in the voting for the Most Valuable Player award.

Tony led the Padres to a 92-70 record and the NL West Division title, only the second time in franchise history the team had even had a winning record for an entire year. The reward was a berth in the League Championship Series against the Chicago Cubs. San Diego fell behind in the series and was facing elimination in the ninth inning of Game 4 when Tony came up to bat.

He singled, which brought Garvey up to bat. Fighting off a stomach virus, Garvey came through in dramatic fashion. His fourth hit of the game was a two-run homer off Lee Smith that broke the 5-5 tie and gave San Diego the victory, extending the series to a fifth and deciding game.

Tony won his first batting title in 1984. (AP/Wide World Photos)

Tony slides safely back to first on a pickoff attempt.
(AP/Wide World Photos)

The Cubs were within three innings of ending their prolonged postseason drought the next night. They led 3-0 entering the sixth and were still on top 3-2 as the game reached the seventh inning. Tony's two-run double, however, was part of a four-run seventh inning that gave San Diego a 6-3 win and its first National League pennant.

Almost nobody in San Diego cared who the Padres had to play in the World Series. Getting there had been the goal, and it had been achieved.

Waiting to oppose the Padres were the Detroit Tigers, who had gone 104-58 in the regular season. They were too strong for the Padres, who also no doubt still were suffering from a little letdown after their playoff victory. The Tigers won the Series in five games.

Tony enjoyed a quality postseason, finishing with a .316 average in 10 games. He had a lot of reasons to be happy, believing there were many more successful seasons ahead. He had no idea then how hard it would be, or how long he would have to wait, to get back to the World Series again.

Tony watches a foul ball off a pitch from Colorado Rockies pitcher Bobby Jones. (AP/Wide World Photos)

The Lean Years

While the Padres fell out of the pennant race for several years, Tony was able to increase his reputation as one of the best hitters in baseball.

He became a favorite not only of fans in San Diego, but around the National League. He won three consecutive batting titles, from 1987 through 1989. His 1987 crown came despite the fact the Padres began the year with a 12-42 record and lost 97 games, the most by the franchise since 1974. If not for Tony's .370 average, it would have been even worse.

A year later, the Padres made a managerial change near midseason from Larry Bowa to Jack McKeon and the club rode a second-half surge to finish with an 83-78 record. That season, Tony batted .313 and won the National League batting title with the lowest average in that league's history, seven points lower than the .320 hit by Larry Doyle for the 1915 New York Giants.

Tony won the silver bat again in 1989 when he and then-San Francisco Giants first baseman Will Clark went into the final weekend of the season in a virtual tie. The two teams faced each other in a three-game season-ending series in San Diego that could have also determined the division title. But the Padres were eliminated in their 159th game on an extra-inning double by then-Cincinnati center fielder Eric Davis.

Tony Gwynn

n eight National League batting titles in
gue career. (AP/Wide World Photos)

*As the years passed, Tony became more focused on getting
his team to the World Series. (AP/Wide World Photos)*

Tony went 6-for-8 in the final series and, after smacking a single on a Sunday afternoon in San Diego, was congratulated by Clark as he rounded first base to a huge ovation from 22,359 hometown fans. Tony won his third consecutive batting title with a .336 average and led the league with 203 hits. Clark finished at .333 with 196 hits and never again came close to winning a batting title.

Despite the batting titles, Tony was getting tired of losing. He was ready to trade in all of his trophies if it meant having a better chance for the team to reach the World Series.

"As you get older, you start focusing on things other people have done and records other people have set," Tony said. "You forget about why you're here in the first place—and that's to win."

Tony's frustrations increased as the Padres were not successful in becoming a contending team again. Mrs. Joan Kroc, who had taken over the team after

the death of her husband, McDonald's, put the team

In 1990, the team wa ducer Tom Werner and a g nessmen, who had the u coming owners just as baseball were the worst

By 1993, with the P as Joe Carter, Fred Mc other teams, and with as Benito Santiago, Alomar and John K in disarray.

Attendance pl news the fans had 1993 Padres lost 1 that 1974 season, ing about his fut ing counsel and

Tony has wo his major-le

As the years passed, Tony became more focused on getting his team to the World Series. (AP/Wide World Photos)

Tony went 6-for-8 in the final series and, after smacking a single on a Sunday afternoon in San Diego, was congratulated by Clark as he rounded first base to a huge ovation from 22,359 hometown fans. Tony won his third consecutive batting title with a .336 average and led the league with 203 hits. Clark finished at .333 with 196 hits and never again came close to winning a batting title.

Despite the batting titles, Tony was getting tired of losing. He was ready to trade in all of his trophies if it meant having a better chance for the team to reach the World Series.

"As you get older, you start focusing on things other people have done and records other people have set," Tony said. "You forget about why you're here in the first place—and that's to win."

Tony's frustrations increased as the Padres were not successful in becoming a contending team again. Mrs. Joan Kroc, who had taken over the team after the death of her husband, Ray, the founder of McDonald's, put the team up for sale.

In 1990, the team was sold to television producer Tom Werner and a group of San Diego businessmen, who had the unfortunate timing of becoming owners just as the financial problems in baseball were the worst they had ever been.

By 1993, with the Padres scattering players such as Joe Carter, Fred McGriff and Gary Sheffield to other teams, and with homegrown products such as Benito Santiago, brothers Sandy and Roberto Alomar and John Kruk traded, the team appeared in disarray.

Attendance plummeted, and the only positive news the fans had was Tony's performance. The 1993 Padres lost 101 games, their highest total since that 1974 season, and Tony was definitely wondering about his future. His father called often, offering counsel and advice.

*Tony has won eight National League batting titles in
his major-league career. (AP/Wide World Photos)*

What Charles Gwynn was telling his son that perhaps he should think about moving to another team. As a veteran player with 10 years of service in the major leagues, the last five with the same club, Tony had the privilege of saying where he would or would not be traded. He admitted he didn't know what he should do. He wanted to win, but he considered San Diego his home.

"He wanted me to go," Tony said. "He kept saying, 'You deserve better than that.' I tried to explain both sides of the fence. He turned it around and put it back in my lap. He said: 'If you feel like it's time to go then ask them to trade you. But if you feel like you have unfinished business to take care of, hang around. Nobody is going to criticize you for staying someplace where you're happy.'"

Two days later, the phone calls from dad stopped. Tony learned his father had been taken to the hospital with chest pains. A decade earlier, his father had survived a heart attack and had been closely monitored ever since.

This time, Charles Gwynn didn't recover. He died at age 61 on November 27, 1993, the day Tony describes as "the worst day of my life."

Tony now would have to face the challenges ahead without his dad's advice, something he wasn't certain he would be able to do.

Four in a Row

Tony was determined to do the best he could in 1994, knowing that was what his father would expect of him. On the field, he was fine. It was when he had time to think away from the field that made it a long, lonely year.

"It's been tough, especially when I'm by myself and have time to reflect," Tony said. "I can focus on baseball like I always have, but during the course of the day, there's always a time when I'm thinking about not being able to talk, or not being able to see my dad."

Tony knew his dad would have been proud of the way he performed on the field. He won his fifth NL batting title, and first since 1989, with a lofty average of .394. It was the highest average by an NL hitter since Bill Terry hit .401 in 1930 and the highest average in the majors since Ted Williams became the last hitter to top .400 with a .406 average in 1941.

Had the season not been shortened because of a player's strike that wiped out the remaining 45 games, Tony might have had a chance to reach that cherished plateau.

His father's death also hit Tony hard because of other tragedies that had affected some of his friends from earlier days on the Padres.

Former teammate Alan Wiggins died, a victim of AIDS. Third-base coach Jack Krol died of cancer. Pitcher Dave Dravecky lost his arm to a cancerous tumor. When pitcher Eric Show died at age

37 of a drug overdose, it left Tony very depressed.

Show's wife, Cara Mia, asked Tony to attend the funeral in a Riverside, California, church, but his father's death was so fresh, Tony had yet to find the courage even to revisit his dad's grave. The Padres were playing their first spring training in Peoria, Arizona, after 25 springs across the state in Yuma, but he couldn't leave the team.

"I consider Eric Show to be a friend of mine, but I couldn't be there," Tony said at the time. "Not because I was playing baseball, but because mentally I just knew I just couldn't go to another funeral. For that I apologize, but I wasn't ready."

There has been absolutely nothing for Tony to apologize for during his baseball career, and having the troubled 1994 season finally come to an end was a great relief. He came back for the start of the 1995 season ready to attack the game with vigor once more.

Tony hit .350 or better for five consecutive seasons.
(AP/Wide World Photos)

The result was another batting title, this time with an average of .368. He did not go more than two consecutive starts without getting a hit all season. The sixth title equaled the total of Ted Williams, regarded as one of the greatest hitters ever.

Tony has always enjoyed meeting and talking baseball with some of the greatest players in the history of the game, such as Williams and St. Louis great Stan Musial. Williams told Tony he would become a better hitter if he would pull the ball more to right field, which would both increase his power numbers and give him more room to drop in shorter base hits.

Tony tried to follow that advice, and in 1996 produced yet another batting title, his seventh, with a .353 average. It was his fourth consecutive season of hitting .350 or better. Only Ty Cobb, Rogers Hornsby and Al Simmons had posted that high an average for a longer period of time.

Another title, his fourth in a row, with a .372 average followed in 1997, truly establishing Tony as one of the greatest hitters of all-time. From opening day of the 1993 season until the end of the 1997 season, Tony's composite average was .368.

Gwynn's .394 in the strike-shortened 1994 season was the highest batting average to lead the National League since Musial's .376 in 1948. Since Williams batted .406 in 1941, Gwynn has had four of major-league baseball's top eight batting averages. He is among the select company of George Brett, Rod Carew, Musial and Williams, Hall of Famers all of them.

Tony had never been to the shrine in Cooperstown, New York, until the Padres played an exhibition game there in 1997 as part of the Hall of Fame induction weekend ceremonies. It will only be a matter of time before he returns for his own induction.

Greg Maddux of the Atlanta Braves considers Tony the toughest batter in the major leagues. (AP/Wide World Photos)

Until he is ready to retire, however, Tony is going to continue to try to play as well as he can and lead the Padres toward a World Series, which was his goal when the 1998 season began.

CHAPTER EIGHT

Back to the World Series

For the first time in 14 years, since Tony thought winning and getting to the World Series was going to be easy, the Padres finally made it again in 1998.

He batted .321, a six-year low. As always, he was a model of consistency, hitting .320 against right-handed pitchers and .323 against left-handed pitchers.

Atlanta great Greg Maddux, perhaps the best pitcher in the game today, calls Tony the toughest batter in the major leagues.

Yet, Tony was the first to acknowledge that he had disappointed himself and the fans when the Padres romped to a franchise high 98 victories, winning the National League West for the second time in three seasons by nine games.

Tony's old sharpness was not there and at no point in the season did he make one of his signature runs when he hits above .400 for weeks on end. Tony has always worked hard to maintain his consistency, alternately spending long hours in the batting cage and hitting thousands of balls off a stationary tee.

His approach must have worked. Heading into 1998, he was a .323 hitter against left-handers and a .348 hitters against right-handers, a .345 hitter at home and a .334 hitter on the road, a .340 hitter on grass and a .337 hitter on artificial turf, a .332 hitter during the day and a .343 hitter at night.

Gwynn is his own toughest critic, and in the
wake of the Padres' stunning six-game victory over
the Atlanta Braves in the National League Championship Series, he made this assessment of his con-
tribution to the pennant-winning cause: "I stink,"
he said in disappointment. "I admit it. I keep working at it. But I've got to swing the bat a lot better."

Gwynn's words applied to the playoffs and the
entire regular season when he was beset by sore knees
and injuries to his Achilles tendon and thumb, and
missed 35 games. Last season, Gwynn's batting average dropped 51 points, and with it, his string of
four consecutive NL batting titles came to an end.

In the NLCS, Gwynn batted .231, although
he went 2-for-5 against the Braves in the series finale at Turner Field. In the Padres' four-game division series win over Houston, Gwynn batted .200.
Overall in 10 playoff games, he was 9-for-41 with

Tony has played 15 full seasons in the majors. (AP/ Wide World Photos)

three doubles and four runs batted in for a .220 batting average. Gwynn, though, wouldn't blame the injuries.

"It doesn't have anything to do with my stroke," he said. "It was just bad. I'm not going to sit here and try to candy coat it and say I should be better right now. When you're hitting .220 coming into the game, you stink."

Asked if that analysis applied to the entire season, Gwynn responded with his usual candor.

"Pretty much," Gwynn said. "But you see me smiling here, don't you? I'm very happy. I just wasn't as consistent as I want to be. For two months I was right there and then for the next two months I did nothing. I kept asking myself, why? And by the time I figured it out two months had gone by and you go from hitting .370 to hitting .300.

"For me, individually, I can do better and I'm not ashamed to admit that. There are seasons when you do exactly what you want to do. But there are other seasons when you're going to be inconsistent. For me, this year I was very inconsistent. I hope next year I'll be ready to go. The irony is, so what? I'm the happiest I've been in about 10 years because I'm going where I want to go."

That was to a World Series date with the Yankees, a trip to The House that Ruth Built and to Monument Gardens. Gwynn is the only Padre to play on both the 1984 and 1998 pennant-winners, and he was the only one to be on the field for both stunning disappointments.

Manager Bruce Bochy and coaches Tim Flannery and Greg Booker also played on that ill-fated 1984 team that split the first two games against the Detroit Tigers in San Diego and then were demolished in three straight at Tiger Stadium where their pitching abandoned them. The Padres were outscored by the Tigers 23-15.

Gwynn's legacy in that series was a .263 batting average (5-for-19) with no extra base hits and no runs batted in. He took that into Monument Gardens last fall and into his second World Series on the tail of a postseason of despair at the plate.

And then Gwynn locked in, hitting a home run off Yanks left-hander David Wells in Game 1 into the fabled right field seats where Ruth and Mantle and Maris and so many other baseball greats had once deposited baseballs.

For a moment, the Padres showed a glimmer of hope in that game against a team that would win 125 regular and postseason games last season. They were up 5-3 going into the bottom of the seventh. Then Chuck Knoblauch tied the game with a three-run homer and Tino Martinez hit a grand slam. The final was 9-6 and when the Padres lost Game 2, 9-3, in an affair that ended early when the Yankees jumped out to a 7-0, third-inning lead, the series seemed over as it returned to San Diego.

The Padres fought gamely, losing Game 3 5-4 because of two homers by New York third baseman Scott Brosius, the series MVP, and the finale 3-0 when Brosius knocked in another run and gloved the ninth-inning ground ball he tossed to first for the final out.

For Gwynn, the ending was bittersweet. In his two World Series, the Padres had finished 1-8, their lone victory coming in San Diego on October 10, 1984 —a 5-3 victory over the Tigers. But this time Gwynn's bat had come alive. He went 8-for-16 and batted .500 in the series with that home run and three runs batted in.

It was all over as quickly as it had begun and Gwynn couldn't gloat in his accomplishments. He is facing a new era in San Diego, one in which the Padres hope to have a new downtown ballpark near the harbor front convention center by 2002, and the team changed players again. For various reasons during the offseason, the Padres lost stalwarts Kevin Brown, Steve Finley and Ken Caminiti to free agency and traded Joey Hamilton and Greg Vaughn.

Tony waves to the crowd after moving into a tie with Babe Ruth for 32nd place on the all-time hits list. (AP/ Wide World Photos)

CHAPTER NINE

72 Hits Shy of 3,000

But Tony has become weary now, of all the traveling and all the days away from home. Although he has long been the best interview in baseball, he claims that his last interview won't come soon enough. He has always hated flying, tough in a sport where road trips stretch out like beads on a string of pearls. He was chastened last summer when the private jet he was flying in, provided by Padres owner John Moores, nearly crashed when it was caught in a sudden draft of

Tony with his wife, Alicia, during the Padres' post-World Series parade in downtown San Diego. (AP/ Wide World Photos)

wind on its approach into Denver's new airport just before the All-Star game at Coors Field.

"I've said that as long as the game is fun I'd still like to play, but I'm tired of all the hassles," said Gwynn, who will be 39 before the current season is over. "The airplane flights and hotels. I'm tired of all of it. I've said I wanted to play until I'm 40, but I don't have to, and that's a good thing. I'm one of those lucky guys who can say when I've had enough.

"I still love to play the game and when I'm out there I block it all out, but everything else—talking about it every day—you can have it. And I really mean that. I told my wife and kids and they understand. They know where I'm coming from."

He has his long-term health to think about after a string of leg injuries, plus there is his family legacy of heart problems.

Since his father's death, his health, his weight, and his family heredity have become major con-

***Tony smiles during practice at Yankee Stadium before
the 1998 World Series. (AP/Wide World Photos)***

cerns. His mother, now 65, has suffered a heart attack of her own. He is a prisoner of his body and his own bad habits. Eight years ago, a tumor tangled among the lymph nodes was removed from his neck below the right ear. The tumor proved to be benign.

For the umpteenth time in his 16-year career, Gwynn is facing another Padres face lift. This time, he's also facing his milestone 3,000th hit and the end of the line. He would be 42 by the time the new ballpark is open and he only has two years remaining on his contract.

"I can be a fan and sit in a new ballpark and enjoy it just like everybody else," he said. "It could be time to pack it in and shut it down. People in this organization will be crushed. But I don't have to play that long."

Tony Gwynn Quick Facts

Full Name:	Anthony Keith Gwynn
Team:	San Diego Padres
Hometown:	Los Angeles, California
Position:	Outfielder
Jersey Number:	19
Bats:	Left
Throws:	Left
Height:	5-11
Weight:	215 pounds
Birthdate:	May 9, 1960

1998 Highlight: Though his .321 average was his lowest since 1992, it marked the 16th consecutive season he's hit better than .300

Stats Spotlight: Needs just 72 hits in 1999 to become the 22nd player to record 3,000 or more career hits

Little-Known Fact: Joined baseball immortal Honus Wagner as only players in history to win eight National League batting titles

Batters with 3,000 hits

	Player	Hits
1.	Pete Rose	4,256
2.	Ty Cobb	4,191
3.	Hank Aaron	3,771
4.	Stan Musial	3,630
5.	Tris Speaker	3,515
6.	Honus Wagner	3,430
7.	Carl Yastrzemski	3,419
8.	Paul Molitor	3,319
9.	Eddie Collins	3,313
10.	Willie Mays	3,283
11.	Eddie Murray	3,255

Batters with 3,000 hits cont.

12.	Nap Lajoie	3,251
13.	George Brett	3,154
14.	Paul Waner	3,152
15.	Robin Yount	3,142
16.	Dave Winfield	3,110
17.	Rod Carew	3,053
18.	Cap Anson	3,041
19.	Lou Brock	3,023
20.	Al Kaline	3,007
21.	Roberto Clemente	3,000

Tony Gwynn's Professional Career

Year	Club	AVG	G	AB	R	H	2B	3B	HR	RBI	BB	SO	SB
1981	Walla Walla	.331*	42	178	46	59	12	1	12	37	23	21	17
	Amarillo	.462	23	91	22	42	8	2	4	19	5	7	5
1982	Hawaii	.328	93	366	65	120	23	2	5	46	18	18	14
	San Diego	.289	54	190	33	55	12	2	1	17	14	16	8
1983	Las Vegas	.342	17	73	15	25	6	0	0	7	6	5	3
	San Diego	.309	86	304	34	94	12	2	1	37	23	21	7
1984	San Diego	.351*	158	606	88	213*	21	10	5	71	59	23	33
1985	San Diego	.317	154	622	90	197	29	5	6	46	45	33	14
1986	San Diego	.329	160	642	107	#211*	33	7	14	59	52	35	37
1987	San Diego	.370*	157	589	119	218*	36	13	7	54	82	35	56
1988	San Diego	.313*	133	521	64	163	22	5	7	70	51	40	26
1989	San Diego	.336*	158	604	82	203*	27	7	4	62	56	30	40
1990	San Diego	.309	141	573	79	177	29	10	4	72	44	23	17
1991	San Diego	.317	134	530	69	168	27	11	4	62	34	19	8
1992	San Diego	.317	128	520	77	165	27	3	6	41	46	16	3
1993	San Diego	.358	122	489	70	175	41	3	7	59	36	19	14
1994	San Diego	.394*	110	419	79	165*	35	1	12	64	48	19	5
1995	San Diego	.368*	135	535	82	197#	33	1	9	90	35	15	17
1996	San Diego	.353*	116	451	67	159	27	2	3	50	39	17	11
1997	San Diego	.372*	149	592	97	220*	49	2	17	119	43	28	12
1998	San Diego	.321	127	461	65	148	35	0	16	69	35	18	3
Padres Totals		.339	2222	8648	1302	2928	495	84	123	1042	742	407	311

*Led League   #Tied for League Lead

***Tony circles the bases after homering off David Wells.
(AP/Wide World Photos)***

1990s Hits Leaders

Tony Gwynn	**1574**
Mark Grace	1571
Paul Molitor	1568
Rafael Palmeiro	1564
Craig Biggio	1540

Active Hits Leaders

Tony Gwynn	**2928**
Wade Boggs	2922
Cal Ripken	2878
Rickey Henderson	2678
Harold Baines	2649
Tim Raines	2532
Chili Davis	2252
Gary Gaetti	2223
Willie McGee	2186

Active Career Batting Leaders

Tony Gwynn	**.339**
Mike Piazza	.333
Wade Boggs	.329
Frank Thomas	.321
Edgar Martinez	.318
Alex Rodriguez	.313
Kenny Lofton	.311
Rusty Greer	.310
Mark Grace	.310
Nomar Garciaparra	.309

Consecutive Batting Titles

Player	Titles	Seasons
Ty Cobb	9	1907-1915
Rogers Hornsby	6	1920-1925
Tony Gwynn	**4**	**1994-1997**
Rod Carew	4	1972-1975
Wade Boggs	4	1985-1988

Total Batting Titles in a Career

Player	Titles
Ty Cobb	12
Tony Gwynn	**8**
Honus Wagner	8
Rogers Hornsby	7
Stan Musial	7
Rod Carew	7
Ted Williams	6

Consecutive Seasons as a .300 Hitter

Player	Years	Streak
Ty Cobb	23	1906-1928
Honus Wagner	17	1897-1913
Stan Musial	16	1942-1958
Tony Gwynn	**16**	**1983-1998**
Rod Carew	15	1969-1983
Ted Williams	15	1939-1958

Tony Gwynn's Greatest Hits

Following is a list of Tony Gwynn's most productive games over the last 10 years of his career.

Date	Opp	AB	R	H	2B	3B	HR	RBI
4/03/98	@StL	4	4	3	0	0	0	2
4/22/98	@ChN	5	1	3	0	0	0	0
5/01/98	@Fla	5	1	3	1	0	0	0
5/04/98	@Mil	4	1	3	0	0	0	2
6/05/98	@Tex	5	1	3	2	0	0	0
6/21/98	@SF	4	1	3	1	0	0	1
7/28/98	@NYN	5	1	3	0	0	1	2
7/29/98	@NYN	5	1	4	3	0	0	0

Date	Opp	AB	R	H	2B	3B	HR	RBI
9/01/98	NYN	3	1	3	1	0	0	2
98 Totals		461	65	148	35	0	16	69
4/01/97	NYN	5	2	3	0	0	0	2
4/09/97	PIT	4	1	3	0	0	1	2
4/11/97	@Phi	5	2	3	0	0	0	0
4/16/97	@Pit	5	2	3	0	0	1	1
5/01/97	@NYN	4	0	3	1	0	0	1
5/02/97	MON	5	2	3	0	0	1	2
5/17/97	@Cin	4	1	3	1	0	1	2
5/18/97	@Cin	4	0	3	0	0	0	0
5/20/97	LA	3	3	3	2	0	0	0
5/22/97	LA	4	0	3	0	0	0	1

Date	Opp	AB	R	H	2B	3B	HR	RBI
5/27/97	ATL	5	1	4	1	0	0	0
6/04/97	@Col	5	2	3	0	0	0	0
6/06/97	HOU	5	1	3	0	0	0	2
6/10/97	STL	5	1	3	3	0	0	3
6/23/97	@SF	6	1	3	1	0	0	1
7/01/97	@Oak	5	1	4	0	0	0	2
7/11/97	@Col	5	2	4	0	0	2	3
7/12/97	@Col	5	2	3	1	0	0	2
7/14/97	SF	4	1	3	1	1	0	3
8/23/97	@NYN	4	1	3	1	0	0	0
8/25/97	@Phi	4	0	3	0	0	0	0
9/19/97	SF	5	2	3	2	0	0	1

Date	Opp	AB	R	H	2B	3B	HR	RBI
9/20/97	SF	4	3	3	1	0	0	3
9/22/97	SF	5	1	4	0	0	0	0
97 Totals		592	97	220	49	2	17	119
4/06/96	@ChN	4	1	4	0	0	0	0
4/05/96	@Hou	6	2	3	1	0	0	2
4/06/96	@Hou	5	1	3	0	0	0	1
4/13/96	ATL	4	2	3	1	0	0	0
5/15/96	NYN	4	1	3	0	0	0	1
6/08/96	PIT	5	1	3	1	0	0	1
6/11/96	CIN	5	1	3	0	0	1	1
6/18/96	@Atl	5	0	3	0	0	0	1

Date	Opp	AB	R	H	2B	3B	HR	RBI
6/21/96	CHN	5	1	3	2	0	0	0
6/22/96	CHN	6	2	3	1	0	0	0
6/30/96	@SF	6	2	3	1	0	0	1
8/14/96	@Cin	6	0	3	0	0	0	0
8/17/96	NYN	5	0	3	2	0	0	2
8/21/96	MON	4	1	3	1	0	0	1
8/29/96	@NYN	5	1	3	0	0	0	1
9/04/96	@Phi	4	2	4	1	0	0	0
9/15/96	CIN	4	1	4	0	0	0	2
9/24/96	COL	5	1	3	0	0	0	0
9/25/96	COL	4	1	3	2	0	0	0
96 Totals		451	67	159	27	2	3	50

Date	Opp	AB	R	H	2B	3B	HR	RBI
4/30/95	CIN	4	2	3	0	0	0	1
5/03/95	@Col	5	2	3	0	0	0	1
5/09/95	LA	4	1	3	0	0	0	3
5/28/95	@Phi	5	3	3	0	0	0	2
5/31/95	@NYN	5	0	3	1	0	0	0
6/04/95	MON	4	1	4	0	0	0	2
6/06/95	PHI	3	0	3	1	0	0	0
6/25/95	COL	5	1	3	0	0	1	2
6/28/95	@LA	4	2	3	1	0	0	0
7/04/95	@Fla	5	1	3	1	0	0	1
7/06/95	@Hou	5	0	3	1	0	0	2
7/08/95	@Hou	7	0	3	1	0	0	1

Date	Opp	AB	R	H	2B	3B	HR	RBI
7/30/95	HOU	4	1	3	1	0	0	0
7/31/95	HOU	3	0	3	0	0	0	3
8/02/95	SF	5	2	3	0	0	0	1
9/03/95	PHI	4	0	3	0	0	0	1
9/04/95	NYN	5	0	3	1	0	0	0
9/06/95	NYN	3	1	3	0	0	0	0
9/09/95	@Stl	5	1	3	0	0	0	1
9/16/95	CHN	5	1	3	0	0	0	3
9/19/95	COL	4	3	3	0	0	0	0
9/22/95	@LA	5	1	3	0	0	0	0
9/25/95	@SF	5	1	3	1	0	0	2

Date	Opp	AB	R	H	2B	3B	HR	RBI
9/29/95	LA	4	2	3	1	0	1	2
95 Totals		535	82	197	33	1	9	90
4/16/94	@StL	5	1	3	2	0	0	0
4/21/94	MON	4	1	3	1	0	0	0
4/23/94	PHI	5	4	5	1	0	1	3
4/24/94	PHI	4	2	3	0	0	0	0
5/06/94	COL	4	3	3	0	0	0	0
5/11/94	CIN	5	2	3	0	1	0	0
5/13/94	@LA	4	2	3	1	0	1	1
5/14/94	@LA	4	0	3	1	0	0	0
6/11/94	@SF	5	1	4	0	0	0	0
6/21/94	LA	5	1	3	0	0	0	2

Date	Opp	AB	R	H	2B	3B	HR	RBI
7/02/94	NYN	4	0	3	1	0	0	3
7/16/94	@NYN	5	1	3	2	0	0	0
7/17/94	@NYN	4	2	3	1	0	0	0
7/22/94	@Phi	5	1	4	0	0	0	1
8/02/94	@LA	4	2	3	1	0	0	0
8/07/94	@ChN	5	1	3	1	0	1	2
8/11/94	@Hou	5	2	3	0	0	0	0
94 Totals		419	79	165	35	1	12	64

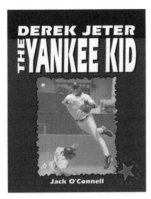

Derek Jeter: The Yankee Kid

Author: Jack O'Connell
ISBN: 1-58261-043-6

In 1996 Derek burst onto the scene as one of the most promising young shortstops to hit the big leagues in a long time. His hitting prowess and ability to turn the double play have definitely fulfilled the early predictions of greatness.

A native of Kalamazoo, MI, Jeter has remained well grounded. He patiently signs autographs and takes time to talk to the young fans who will be eager to read more about him in this book.

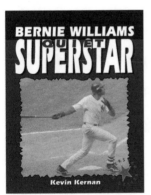

Bernie Williams: Quiet Superstar

Author: Kevin Kernan
ISBN: 1-58261-044-4

Bernie Williams, a guitar-strumming native of Puerto Rico, is not only popular with his teammates, but is considered by top team officials to be the heir to DiMaggio and Mantle fame.

He draws frequent comparisons to Roberto Clemente, perhaps the greatest player ever from Puerto Rico. Like Clemente, Williams is humble, unassuming, and carries himself with quiet dignity. Also like Clemente, he plays with rare determination and a special elegance. He's married, and serves as a role model not only for his three children, but for his young fans here and in Puerto Rico.

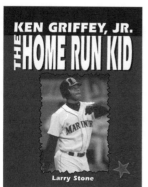

Ken Griffey, Jr.: The Home Run Kid

Author: Larry Stone
ISBN: 1-58261-041-x

Capable of hitting majestic home runs, making breathtaking catches, and speeding around the bases to beat the tag by a split second, Ken Griffey, Jr. is baseball's Michael Jordan. Amazingly, Ken reached the Major Leagues at age 19, made his first All-Star team at 20, and produced his first 100 RBI season at 21.

The son of Ken Griffey, Sr., Ken is part of the only father-son combination to play in the same outfield together in the same game, and, like Barry Bonds, he's a famous son who turned out to be a better player than his father.

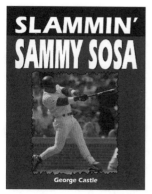

Sammy Sosa: Slammin' Sammy

Author: George Castle
ISBN: 1-58261-029-0

1998 was a break-out year for Sammy as he amassed 66 home runs, led the Chicago Cubs into the playoffs and finished the year with baseball's ultimate individual honor, MVP.

When the national spotlight was shone on Sammy during his home run chase with Mark McGwire, America got to see what a special person he is. His infectious good humor and kind heart have made him a role model across the country.

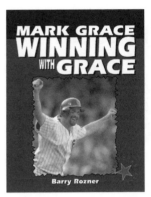

Mark Grace: Winning with Grace

Author: Barry Rozner
ISBN: 1-58261-056-8

This southern California native and San Diego State alumnus has been playing baseball in the windy city for nearly fifteen years. Apparently the cold hasn't affected his game. Mark is an all-around player who can hit to all fields and play great defense.

Mark's outgoing personality has allowed him to evolve into one of Chicago's favorite sons. He is also community minded and some of his favorite charities include the Leukemia Society of America and Easter Seals.

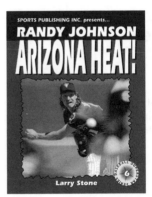

Randy Johnson: Arizona Heat!

Author: Larry Stone
ISBN: 1-58261-042-8

One of the hardest throwing pitchers in the Major Leagues, and, at 6'10" the tallest, the towering figure of Randy Johnson on the mound is an imposing sight which strikes fear into the hearts of even the most determined opposing batters.

Perhaps the most amazing thing about Randy is his consistency in recording strikeouts. He is one of only four pitchers to lead the league in strikeouts for four consecutive seasons. With his recent signing with the Diamondbacks, his career has been rejuvenated and he shows no signs of slowing down.

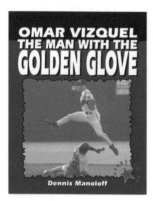

Dennis Manoloff

Omar Vizquel: The Man with the Golden Glove

Author: Dennis Manoloff
ISBN: 1-58261-045-2

Omar has a career fielding percentage of .982 which is the highest career fielding percentage for any shortstop with at least 1,000 games played.

Omar is a long way from his hometown of Caracas, Venezuela, but his talents as a shortstop put him at an even greater distance from his peers while he is on the field.

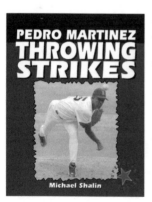

Michael Shalin

Pedro Martinez: Throwing Strikes

Author: Mike Shalin
ISBN: 1-58261-047-9

The 1997 National League Cy Young Award winner is always teased because of his boyish looks. He's sometimes mistaken for the batboy, but his curve ball and slider leave little doubt that he's one of the premier pitchers in the American League.

It is fitting that Martinez is pitching in Boston, where the passion for baseball runs as high as it does in his native Dominican Republic.

Nomar Garciaparra: High 5!

Author: Mike Shalin
ISBN: 1-58261-053-3

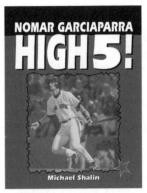

An All-American at Georgia Tech, a star on the 1992 U.S. Olympic Team, the twelfth overall pick in the 1994 draft, and the 1997 American League Rookie of the Year, Garciaparra has exemplified excellence on every level.

At shortstop, he'll glide deep into the hole, stab a sharply hit grounder, then throw out an opponent on the run. At the plate, he'll uncoil his body and deliver a clutch double or game-winning homer. Nomar is one of the game's most complete players.

Juan Gonzalez: Juan Gone!

Author: Evan Grant
ISBN: 1-58261-048-7

One of the most prodigious and feared sluggers in the major leagues, Gonzalez was a two-time home run king by the time he was 24 years old.

After having something of a personal crisis in 1996, the Puerto Rican redirected his priorities and now says baseball is the third most important thing in his life after God and family.

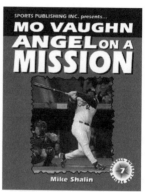

Mo Vaughn:
Angel on a Mission
Author: Mike Shalin
ISBN: 1-58261-046-0

Growing up in Connecticut, this Angels slugger learned the difference between right and wrong and the value of honesty and integrity from his parents early on, lessons that have stayed with him his whole life.

This former American League MVP was so active in Boston charities and youth programs that he quickly became one of the most popular players ever to don the Red Sox uniform. Mo will be a welcome addition to the Angels line-up and the Anaheim community.

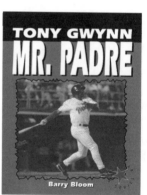

Tony Gwynn:
Mr. Padre
Author: Barry Bloom
ISBN: 1-58261-049-5

Tony is regarded as one of the greatest hitters of all-time. He is one of only three hitters in baseball history to win eight batting titles (the others: Ty Cobb and Honus Wagner).

In 1995 he won the Branch Rickey Award for Community Service by a major leaguer. He is unfailingly humble and always accessible, and he holds the game in deep respect. A throwback to an earlier era, Gwynn makes hitting look effortless, but no one works harder at his craft.

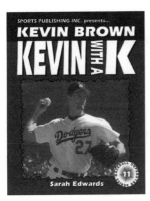

Kevin Brown:
That's Kevin with a "K"
Author: Jacqueline Salman
ISBN: 1-58261-050-9

Kevin was born in McIntyre, Georgia and played college baseball for Georgia Tech. Since then he has become one of baseball's most dominant pitchers and when on top of his game, he is virtually unhittable.

Kevin transformed the Florida Marlins and San Diego Padres into World Series contenders in consecutive seasons, and now he takes his winning attitude and talent to the Los Angeles Dodgers.

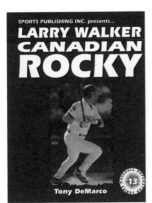

Larry Walker:
Canadian Rocky
Author: Tony DeMarco
ISBN: 1-58261-052-5

Growing up in Canada, Larry had his sights set on being a hockey player. He was a skater, not a slugger, but when a junior league hockey coach left him off the team in favor of his nephew, it was hockey's loss and baseball's gain.

Although the Rockies' star is known mostly for his hitting, he has won three Gold Glove awards, and has worked hard to turn himself into a complete, all-around ballplayer. Larry became the first Canadian to win the MVP award.

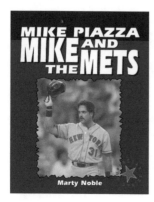

Mike Piazza:
Mike and the Mets
Author: Marty Noble
ISBN: 1-58261-051-7

A total of 1,389 players were selected ahead of Mike Piazza in the 1988 draft, who wasn't picked until the 62nd round, and then only because Tommy Lasorda urged the Dodgers to take him as a favor to his friend Vince Piazza, Mike's father.

Named in the same breath with great catchers of another era like Bench, Dickey and Berra, Mike has proved the validity of his father's constant reminder "If you work hard, dreams do come true."

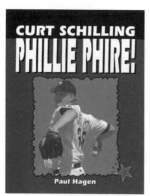

Curt Schilling:
Phillie Phire!
Author: Paul Hagen
ISBN: 1-58261-055-x

Born in Anchorage, Alaska, Schilling has found a warm reception from the Philadelphia Phillies faithful. He has amassed 300+ strikeouts in the past two seasons and even holds the National League record for most strikeouts by a right handed pitcher at 319.

This book tells of the difficulties Curt faced being traded several times as a young player, and how he has been able to deal with off-the-field problems.

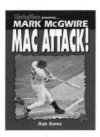

Mark McGwire: Mac Attack!

Author: Rob Rains
ISBN: 1-58261-004-5

Mac Attack! describes how McGwire overcame poor eyesight and various injuries to become one of the most revered hitters in baseball today. He quickly has become a legendary figure in St. Louis, the home to baseball legends such as Stan Musial, Lou Brock, Bob Gibson, Red Schoendienst and Ozzie Smith. McGwire thought about being a police officer growing up, but he hit a home run in his first Little League at-bat and the rest is history.

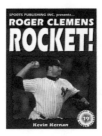

Roger Clemens: Rocket!

Author: Kevin Kernan
ISBN: 1-58261-128-9

When it comes to dominance, few pitchers in baseball history compare to Yankees' fireballer Roger Clemens. Kevin Kernan offers this look at Clemens, and how all of his individual achievements would have so much more meaning with a World Series Ring.

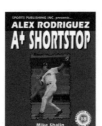

Alex Rodriguez: A+ Shortstop

ISBN: 1-58261-104-1

A-Rod has turned himself into one of the most electrifying players in baseball. This look at the Mariners' All-Star details his success, including his American League record in 1998 of 42 home runs for a shortstop, and his membership in the exclusive 40-40 club.

SUPERSTAR SERIES

Collect Them All!

_____ **Sandy and Roberto Alomar: Baseball Brothers**

_____ **Kevin Brown: Kevin with a "K"**

_____ **Roger Clemens: Rocket!**

_____ **Juan Gonzalez: Juan Gone!**

_____ **Mark Grace: Winning With Grace**

_____ **Ken Griffey, Jr.: The Home Run Kid**

_____ **Tony Gwynn: Mr. Padre**

_____ **Derek Jeter: The Yankee Kid**

_____ **Randy Johnson: Arizona Heat!**

_____ **Pedro Martinez: Throwing Strikes**

_____ **Mike Piazza: Mike and the Mets**

_____ **Alex Rodriguez: A-plus Shortstop**

_____ **Curt Schilling: Philly Phire!**

_____ **Sammy Sosa: Slammin' Sammy**

_____ **Mo Vaughn: Angel on a Mission**

_____ **Omar Vizquel: The Man with a Golden Glove**

_____ **Larry Walker: Canadian Rocky**

_____ **Bernie Williams: Quiet Superstar**

_____ **Mark McGwire: Mac Attack!**

SP
SPORTS
PUBLISHING
INC.

Available by calling 877-424-BOOK